JESUS' GOSPEL OF GOD'S LOVE

Eva Peck

© 2015 by Eva Peck
All rights reserved
Except for any fair dealing permitted under the Copyright Act, no part of this book may be reproduced by any means without prior permission of the author and publisher.

Graphic and cover design: Eva Peck
Cover graphics: Courtesy of SOMMAI and panuruangjan at FreeDigitalPhotos.net
Author photo: Jindrich (Henry) Degen

Bible quotes are taken from the *Holy Bible, New International Version*. Copyright © 1973, 1978, 1984 by International Bible Society. Used by permission of Zondervan Publishing House. All rights reserved.

National Library of Australia Cataloguing-in-Publication entry

Creator: Peck, Eva, author.
Title: Jesus' gospel of God's love / Eva Peck.

ISBN: 9780992454944 (paperback)

Subjects: Bible--History.
Bible--Criticism, interpretation, etc.
Christianity.

Dewey Number: 220.6

This book can be purchased online through
http://www.pathway-publishing.org.
Also available at Amazon, Ingram, and other outlets worldwide.

Dedicated to
our Loving Heavenly Father
and my present and future friends
in the Divine Love Community.

Other Books by the Same Author

Divine Reflections in Times and Seasons
Divine Reflections in Natural Phenomena
Divine Reflections in Living Things
Divine Insights from Human Life

Co-author of:
Pathway to Life – Through the Holy Scriptures
Journey to the Divine Within – Through Silence, Stillness and Simplicity

Readers' Comments

This is the book I've been looking for to share with my Christian friends who are devout students of the Bible. My favorite chapter is Jesus' Life and Message of Salvation as my soul soared with inspiration in the greatness of Jesus' mission on earth as I read it. Eva's balanced, non-denominational understanding is supported by scripture references. Her invitation to experience the silence, stillness and simplicity speaks to me, as does her provoking description of how each individual soul is in a battle between sin and righteousness. Overcoming one's sins and the way to purifying one's soul, finding the greatest Gift of God's Divine Love as Eva has done, is for me, THE most important story worth telling in this world! Eva has done a superb job in describing that the way to personal salvation is through the mighty blessing of receiving the Divine Love, rather than by the vicarious atonement through Jesus' death on the cross.
~ Jeanne Fike, Divine Love Sanctuary Foundation,
British Columbia, Canada

Eva Peck has given us a gift with her book *Jesus' Gospel of God's Love*. In this articulate, elegantly written book, Eva highlights the central message of the historical

Jesus. She draws on her rich life experiences and her familiarity with many faith traditions and diverse cultures to contextualize the teachings of the Bible in ways that respect its value in transforming the consciousness of many, while recognizing its limitations. Her scholarship allows her to make a clear, seamless argument which reveals that Jesus' ultimate revelation and central teaching is that of God's Love as the way to salvation, the path to God's Kingdom and at-onement with Him. She answers many key spiritual questions and links the principles of quantum physics with spiritual beliefs, showing the compatibility of science with theology. Her book is a great resource both to students of the Bible and those who, like myself, are unfamiliar with its teachings. Her clarity and ease of expression are evidence of Eva's depth of understanding of the subject material. In this book, she shares with us the insights made possible by the spiritual maturity of her own soul. I highly recommend this book!
~ Terry Adler, Divine Love Sanctuary Foundation, British Columbia, Canada

Finally there is a book that helps me understand the discrepancies found in the Bible and how to deal with that in my own spiritual journey. The author beautifully describes her spiritual journey as it relates to the Bible and shows how some Bible teachings simply do not make sense when taking into consideration the beliefs of the

Hebrew people during the time of Jesus. Furthermore, the author clearly shows that the Bible still contains many wonderful truths which have helped so many people develop a relationship with God. I highly recommend this book to anyone who would like an enlightened understanding of the origin of the Bible and the spiritual treasures that it contains.

~ Rev. Dr. Michael Nedbal, Trustee of Foundation Church of Divine Truth, Hawaii, USA

This book is an important document rich in truth. It takes the reader incrementally through a journey of understanding the fundamental concepts which are the building blocks to understanding what Divine Love is. The author does so by effectively weaving biblical and scientific understanding with revelations in the Padgett materials so as to present a viable and comprehensive study of spiritual truth. It is beautifully written and thoughtfully presented. I would heartily recommend this book to anyone be they Christian or otherwise. It presents a powerful alternative to orthodox and outdated Christian thought. It's a firecracker of a book, bound to open the eyes of the most conservative thinker on the subject.

~ Al Fike, Divine Love Sanctuary Foundation, British Columbia, Canada

Readers' Comments

Eva Peck has given the world a gift with the book *Jesus' Gospel of God's Love*. Ms. Peck is a master of biblical knowledge and she puts this knowledge to perfect use as she shows us how important divine revelations received 100 years ago align very well with quotations direct from Scripture. Are there two spiritual paths being presented in the Bible? Is one correct and the other incorrect? Eva Peck discusses these questions, biblical history, and many other spiritual matters in this informative book about Divine Love, Jesus Christ, the Holy Bible and human destiny.
~ Brian M. Holmes, writer and editor, New Jersey, USA

If you're searching for more meaning in your life and a fresh perspective of the Bible, you have found the right book. Eva Peck, with her in-depth knowledge of the Bible and biblical history, will guide you to a hidden treasure that runs through the Bible like a golden thread; hidden but not so to the curious and open minded searcher. This treasure is the greatest gift offered by God in all of His creation. It is His Divine Love. Eva explains how and why this knowledge was hidden after Jesus Christ revealed it to his disciples over 2000 years ago. Seek and you shall find, knock and the door will be opened. With each turn of the page, Eva opens the door a little more and will set you upon a spiritual journey unlike anything you could have imagined in your wildest dreams. A journey that will take you to the very Kingdom of God and a relationship with your Heavenly Father that will grow so strong that you

Readers' Comments

will feel Him at the very core of your being, heart and soul. Eva Peck will take your hand and guide you page by page, step by step to this priceless Pearl that Jesus Christ proclaimed – God's peace that passes all understanding (Philippians 4:7).

~ David Reed, Montana, USA

Eva Peck's interesting and informative book presents a lot of material in such an abbreviated and simplified way that it does not overwhelm the reader. To me, this book can be compared to an artist drawing a picture that is a beautiful masterpiece. Eva's unique background of having belonged to a non-traditional church, coupled with her theological education, as well as writing and editing skills – plus having experienced receiving the Pentecostal shower, has truly equipped her for such a time as this. This book is a perfect example of Eva's ability and spiritual understanding to bridge the gap between the Divine Love community and those coming out of organized religion who can look up to and respect her and her work. I enjoyed the book.

~ Marga McCrady, California, USA

I really like what you wrote. It is a very fast read and is a perfect book for those who are looking beyond the Christian faith for higher truths.

~ Joan Warden, author, California, USA

Contents

Introduction 1

Chapter 1: The Bible and Development of Christianity 4

Chapter 2: Nature of God 13

Chapter 3: Early History and Human Origins 16

Chapter 4: Natural Human State and Origin of Evil 20

Chapter 5: Beyond Death 24

Chapter 6: Jesus' Life and Message of Salvation 29

Chapter 7: Prayer for Divine Love 35

Chapter 8: Divine Love versus Natural Love 38

Chapter 9: Divine Love in the Bible 42

Chapter 10: Immortal Divine Angels 51

Epilogue 54

Notes and Further Reading 57

References 71

About the Author 72

More About the Author's Other Books 74

Acknowledgments 77

About Pathway Publishing 78

Introduction

We each have unique backgrounds and life experiences shaped to a large degree by when and where we were born, who our parents were, and what circumstances influenced us. These elements have also determined our spiritual journey. This book is in some ways the culmination of my spiritual journey to this point. It shows my latest thinking and what presently resonates with me as the truth of our human potential and destiny. It is presented here in a nutshell for the reader's consideration.

My spiritual journey has been in some ways unique (of course, we all have unique journeys in our own ways), and I believe it has prepared me for where I am now. I spent about 30 years in a non-mainstream exclusive church which had a heavy Bible emphasis, as well as encouraging members to build an individual relationship with God through a discipline of twice daily prayer and daily spiritual reading. The church also felt that it had unique truths (many different from the orthodox beliefs), and hence regarded itself as a notch above other Christians.

After that, over the last two decades, I was led to slowly abandon my exclusive and limited thinking as I was exposed to other groups and ideas – both Christian and of other faiths. It wasn't just an intellectual pursuit for the sake of satisfying curiosity, it was an unmistakable guidance through life's circumstances. With this background I was then led (again, no doubt guided) to what this book is about – Jesus' gospel of God's Love.

About a year ago, through a series of what I believe were guided circumstances, I came across a book under the title *Angelic Revelations of Divine Truth*. As I started reading, the information resonated with me. It spoke about God, Jesus, and human salvation from a different angle, and even though it challenged some of the traditional Christian ideas as well as several of my own beliefs, it made a lot of sense.

The book I found led me to confirm from another angle what I had realized before – the Bible contains intertwining ideas from various sources and not all of them correspond to the teachings of Jesus and the early Christians. There is still much truth in the Bible, but being both the inspired Word of God, as well as a compiled, edited and re-edited creation of men, there are errors and inaccuracies.

The book that you are holding in your hands presents in a succinct way what I now see as closer to Jesus' original teaching regarding the Kingdom of God and salvation. More information can be found on my website www.universal-spirituality.org, in the *Notes and Further Reading* at the end of the book (where key Bible verses, superscripted in the text, are quoted and other online reading referenced), as well as in the list of *References*.

Introduction

While these concepts are not commonly believed and taught by Christian ministers, it is definitely one of the several threads running through the New Testament as is shown in Chapter 9. It has, however, been somewhat lost among other threads and concepts introduced in the selecting, copying and editing processes of the early manuscripts which took place in compiling the biblical canon.

Let's start by exploring the history and nature of the Bible and the development of Christianity. We'll then look at the nature of God, nature of humanity, the afterlife, and the way to achieve our maximum human potential and immortality – in other words, salvation. (Note that for simplicity, God is referred to by the pronoun He, but it is understood that God is genderless and can be regarded as both our Heavenly Father and Mother.)

I believe that you'll find this book an interesting, enriching, and potentially life-changing journey.

Eva Peck,
June, 2015

Chapter 1: The Bible and Development of Christianity

The Bible as the Word of God

Many Christians believe that the Holy Scriptures, or the Bible, are the inspired Word of God in written form. The Scriptures can be viewed as divine communication or self-disclosure to humanity. They identify God as the Creator and Sustainer of all things, and are an invitation to a relationship with this transcendent Being. They include information unattainable through science or reason, addressing life's ultimate questions, such as the purpose of life and the hereafter.

However, the Bible is not literally the Word of God – its contents weren't just dictated by God for individuals to write down word for word. Nevertheless, the book expresses, sometimes in metaphor or in the words of human instruments reflecting their culture and personality, God's past, present and future actions.

God-given inspiration is affirmed in the pages of the Bible itself. Phrases such as "the word of the Lord came to me" appear numerous times and indicate that some of the Old Testament writers knew that they were commissioned by God to write what they did. New Testament writers affirmed the inspiration of the Old Testament writings – the only Scriptures they had – referring to them as the words of God pertaining to historical and prehistoric realities (for example, 1 Kings 12:22; Jer. 18:5[(1)]; Hebr. 11:7[(2)]).

Jesus too affirmed the divine inspiration and authority of the Old Testament. Calling the Scriptures the "word that comes from the mouth of God", he quoted various passages to refer to himself and to predict his death, burial, and resurrection. He also spoke about significant events and persons mentioned in the Old Testament as past realities. After his resurrection, Jesus used Scriptures to show his disillusioned disciples that he was indeed the prophesied Messiah (for example, Matt. 4:4; Luke 17:26-27; 24:13-27[(3)]).

Because of the limitations of language and the incompatibility between language as a human phenomenon and God as Divine Spirit, some have suggested exploring the term "Word of God" as also metaphorical. This allows many concepts to have both a literal and metaphorical meaning, and to be interpreted at several levels. It makes room for imagination to search for depths of meaning beyond the literal. As a result, it enables a range of interpretations and insights, which are also influenced by the understanding, experiences, and prejudices that readers bring to their Bible reading and study. The Holy Bible, like other spiritual writings, remains a living word for people around the world – a treasure chest with endless possibilities of new discoveries.

How the Bible Came to Us

The Bible, while undoubtedly inspired, is also a very human document. It was written over a period spanning fifteen hundred years by people from different walks of life, different time periods, different locations, and in three different languages. It has since been translated into hundreds of modern languages. The writers wrote in their own style, influenced by their background, education, culture, and political situation of the time. Using a range of literary genres, they compiled legal precepts and histories; recorded their joys, sorrows, frustrations, and praises addressed to God; recounted stories; wrote epic poetry; and verbalized dramatic symbolic dreams and visions. New Testament writers interpreted the Old Testament in light of the life of Jesus and their own experiences. A large part of this re-interpretation of the scriptures included confirming Jesus' messiahship and making sense out of his unexpected and shocking death. In trying to do this, texts were sometimes seen as messianic though in reality they may have applied only to the time in which they were written.

Furthermore, the Bible is the product of a complex process of document selection, copying, editing, compilation, and translation – all human activities subject to error. Those who allegedly reproduced the originals (now no longer in existence) added and took away ideas according to their own understanding and motives. As a result, false teachings have been interpolated. There are also intertwining strands of teachings from various sources, and even contradictions. Because of these factors and the complexity of the canonization process, the Bible is a set of writings with great diversity and not always true to the inspired teachings that Jesus brought from the Father.

It is a well-documented fact that the New Testament wasn't finalized until the 4th century – a full 300 years after Jesus' death. At that time the church was recognized as the official religion and came under the control of the Roman Emperor Constantine with the pope and a hierarchy of clergy under him. Because of different strands of Christian beliefs existing side by side – by that time, Christianity was not just a unified set of beliefs – several church councils were called by the emperor to establish orthodox beliefs for the purpose of enforcing unity. More often than not, doctrines were decided following long debates spanning decades or longer. There was never just one opinion on such matters as the nature of Jesus Christ and of the Holy Spirit. However, the idea that most of the attending clergy agreed with became the official orthodox doctrine sanctioned by the emperor. At the same time, other ideas (equally or more valid) were branded as heresies. As time went on, the popes and cardinals of the state-controlled Roman church also introduced non-biblical, even pagan, ideas, such as the Trinity, celibacy for the clergy, purgatory, indulgences (payment for supposedly shortening time in the purgatory), and others.

Despite these limitations, the Bible is still a book that has inspired millions, pointed them to their Creator, and set them on the way to salvation. Without the guidance and inspiration of the Spirit of God within the vast and varied range of human endeavours, such result would be highly unlikely to be achieved by humans alone. The inspiration of the Holy Scriptures is further attested to by the fulfilment of prophecies; the confirmation by history, archaeology, and science; and above all, the changed lives of individuals. Through the message of the Bible, people from all levels of society have been led from darkness to light, received new life, and become transformed.

Further Development of Christianity

Beside the church in Rome under the jurisdiction of Emperor Constantine and his successors, a differing strand of Christianity existed in the East (Turkey, Syria and spreading as far as China at one time). These Christians felt that they had retained the original teachings of Jesus and his disciples and called themselves Orthodox. Besides these, numerous other groups, often persecuted by the official church and forced to flee to deserts and mountains, gathered for group worship with their own understanding.

As Christianity spread to various parts of the world, it changed the prevailing culture, but also adapted itself to it – sometimes absorbing untruths and elements of paganism. In the 16th century, a few courageous men, aware of the corruption in the Roman Catholic Church, stood up and demanded reform. The best-known are Martin Luther in Germany, Ulrich Zwingli in Switzerland, and John (Jean) Calvin, originally from France, who fled to Switzerland from Catholic persecution. But, while they agreed that the Catholic Church needed change, they significantly differed on what the reformed church should look like.

With time, a sizable Protestant movement developed as a result of the reformation attempt. However, with the Scriptures having become available to the lay people, whereas before only the clergy dictated approved dogma, interpretations multiplied. Groups continued to split and there are now thousands of different denominations and sects – each believing they have the truth and that they interpret the Bible correctly.

The Ultimate Revelation

The ultimate divine revelation was in the coming to earth of Jesus Christ who brought the message of God's Divine Love as the way to salvation, the Kingdom of God, and at-onement with the Father. In teaching this vital truth, he also exemplified It by his life (for example, John 17:21-26[4]). This is the crux of this book and one of the threads clearly running through the Bible. It will be explored in subsequent chapters.

Contrary to common beliefs, traditional Christianity as taught by most mainstream churches is, in many aspects, not what was taught by Jesus and the early disciples.

Careful study of the Bible will show that several strands of beliefs are intertwining in its pages – some reflecting early teachings of Jesus' disciples, an alternative form of Christianity, and others added subsequently.

For example, while the Bible asserts in many places that Jesus' blood washes away sins, satisfies the demands of an "angry God", and redeems humanity from eternal suffering, even this was not in the original teachings and writings of those whose names are on the books. Having come from Jewish backgrounds, the disciples would have found the idea of even symbolically drinking blood and eating flesh of their saviour utterly abhorrent based on their Old Testament upbringing, which forbade any consumption of blood (Lev. 17:12-14). An alternative to this teaching is presented as we proceed.

This book strives to uphold the Bible wherever possible, but also draws on less known subsequent revelation from beyond received about a century ago and interpreted by some as Jesus' Second Coming. It has been published under the titles of *True Gospel Revealed Anew by Jesus*, Volumes 1-4, originally published by the Foundation Church of New Birth, and *Angelic Revelations of Divine Truth,* published by the Foundation Church of Divine Truth (see References).

Individual Responsibility

Ultimately, no reasoning or argument can prove the authority, inspiration, and trustworthiness of the Bible or any other writings, or even the existence of a Creator God. Eventually, each person must test for themselves whether the claims of any spiritual writings are true and relevant in today's world, and whether there is a God who answers prayers and helps us in our time of need. These are all matters of faith based on personal experience.

Those who desire to learn about God and to have Him change their life can ask Him to do so. The evidence strongly suggests that earnest petition will be supernaturally and encouragingly answered.

As far as the almost overwhelming choice, and even confusion, among Christian groups, I have come to believe that no church is ideal or perfect (being made of humans, it cannot be). By the same token, no church will teach exactly what each individual believes. Therefore every person needs to find a group where they feel comfortable worshipping and fellowshipping with others of like mind, bearing in mind the above-mentioned limitations.

One key Protestant doctrine in contrast to the Catholic belief is that salvation needs to be worked out by each individual – it is not in the power of the church (Phil. 2:12-15[5]). *Each person is responsible for their own relationship with God and their own salvation.* With that in mind, let's explore with open hearts and minds both the traditional teachings and the alternative ideas that this book proposes. Based on our personal understanding and faith, let us all walk with God to the best of our ability, live by the Golden Rule and Jesus' commandment to love one another as he has loved his disciples, read widely, and hold on what sounds true to us – what speaks to our heart and develops our soul in God's Love.

Chapter 2: Nature of God

God is Soul, composed of His greatest attribute, Divine Love, which is His very nature and essence, followed by mercy, goodness, power, omniscience, and will (1 John 4:8, 16[1]; Psalm 116:12; Deut. 4:31; Eph. 2:4-5[2]). The mind, so much worshipped by humankind, is only one aspect of His Being. God as Soul is far more than the sum of all His attributes.

God's attributes radiate from His great Soul and flood the universe. So, when people say they live and have their being in God (Acts 17:28), they are technically in error, but they do live and have their being in the divine attributes that emanate from God and that He has placed in their human soul. God has a place in the Celestial Heavens, but His attributes are everywhere and fill the whole universe, or multiple universes that scientists postulate might exist. The earth is a tiny portion of the entire universe. Even the "heaven" or spirit world where humans go when they die is a subset of the entirety of Creation (Psalm 47:8[3]; 53:2; 139:7-13[4])

Although God has no form or shape such as He gives to humans on incarnation, nor a spirit body such as that manifested by humans after their physical death, God does possess a Soul form. However, He cannot be seen with the physical or spiritual sight, but can only be perceived with the soul's eyes opened by the influence of the Divine Love. God's form, or its divine attributes, becomes more clearly perceptible to the human soul as it comes into a closer rapport with God. This happens as a result of its development and transformation through the Divine Love (Matt. 5:8; John 3:3; 1 John 3:1-2 [5]).

While God is Soul, alone and unique in its oneness, and while He has no material or spirit body, He has personality – divine personality manifesting His Love, kindness and solicitude for all His creatures. God is a God of Love, above all else. He is not a God of hatred, nor does He chastise His children in wrath or anger. His love is for all humanity, be they saints or sinners, and no one suffers punishment because the Father wants them to suffer. He is a God of mercy and forgiveness, and will forgive the sins of those who in sincerity ask Him (Isa. 55:7[6]).

God, then, is not a cold intellect, an abstract mind, or an indifferent and unfeeling force, but rather a personal, warm and loving Father / Mother, eager for the happiness of His children, regardless of their race, colour or creed. The real truth and meaning of God is beyond the comprehension of the finite mind, and can only be accepted as a realization of an existing truth by means of faith.

No one has ever seen God, for God cannot be seen as described in some of the Bible stories. God generally works through His angels (Heb. 1:14), rather than directly. So His angels and messengers were seen, spoke to the prophets, and represented themselves as angels of God. Jesus was His chosen son to do the work of redeeming the earth from sin, and came as his Father's representative. He never was God, nor did he claim to be (Mark 10:17-18).

No man has heard the voice of God, for He has no voice. The "voice of God" that spoke to the disciples on the Mount of Transfiguration, and to John and those at Jesus' baptism, was actually the voice of one of God's highest angels. Other than communicating through angels or inspired writings, God works in a silent, mysterious way, through communication from His Soul to human souls.

Through His ministering angels, God seeks to turn His children to Him and have them keep in harmony with His laws in developing their natural love, or obtain at-onement with Him through the inflowing of His Divine Love into their souls in response to their earnest prayers. A person can become at-one with the Father to the extent that His Love abounds in their soul. This was what Jesus prayed for in one of his last prayers on earth (John 17:20-23).

Chapter 3: Early History and Human Origins

The Mind beyond Matter

It is now commonly understood, based on the principles of quantum physics, that underneath all matter is energy, and underneath that is a power or force that brings all things into existence – a so-called field of consciousness. The prominent German scientist and contemporary of Albert Einstein, Max Planck, is quoted as saying early in the last century: "All matter originates and exists only by virtue of a force. ... We must assume behind this force the existence of a conscious and intelligent Mind. This Mind is the matrix of all matter."

This mind, matrix, or field of consciousness can also be linked with the transcendent power beyond us or the Source of the elusive subconscious or soul within us. In addition, it can be paralleled with the divine Spirit or Spirit of God, mentioned in the Bible and various sacred texts in the context of creating and executing various tasks. It is the omnipresent life-giving emanation or attribute from the one and only God (who is also referred to as Source, Tao, Great Spirit, Brahmin, Allah, and other names).

This creating and life-giving Spirit – which is not God, but an emanation from God – is the universal energy or life force and consciousness in and behind all things; a kind of a "divine spark" – indeed, in it we (and all else) live, move, and have our being (Acts 17:27-28). From it emanate divine qualities of love, compassion, creativity and expansion, among others. We can choose to align ourselves with these noble qualities and act toward one another in kind, compassionate ways.

This Spirit, mind, or consciousness brought the universe (perhaps multiple universes) into existence. It has been instrumental in the evolution of the universe, having set in motion the cosmic forces creating the innumerable stars, galaxies, and other phenomena. When the time comes for a new order, the Spirit will be involved in destroying the old and creating the new, as well as bringing about other heavenly changes. The ubiquitous Spirit also influences human intellect and moral fibre if humans are open to its benevolent effects (Psalm 139).

Human Origins

What makes humanity unique is a *soul* or *spirit essence* – made in divine image with the potential of being transformed into divine substance (Eccl. 12:6-7[1]; Zech. 12:1[2]). Human-like beings had existed on earth for eons of time, passing, like everything, through a long period of development. At some point they were given a human soul and consciousness. This gave them the realization of being a unique divine creation – in fact the highest and most wonderful of all earthly creatures and objects of God's love and tenderest care.

At the beginning of human history, our ancestors had the opportunity, if their soul so desired, to receive divine nature and reach a state of at-onement with God. This would have been accomplished by asking for and receiving Divine Love through the Holy Spirit, referred to by the prophets in the Old Testament as a *new heart* or *new spirit* (Jer. 24:7; Ezek. 11:19-20[3]; 18:31; 36:26). Instead, however, they rebelled and consequently lost this priceless opportunity. The Divine Love ceased to be available for a long time – till the so called "last days" (Acts 2:17; Heb. 1:2) when Jesus Christ came to earth. He exemplified a life guided by the Divine Love and taught that it was again available to humans for the asking.

After the initial rebellion, referred to as "the Fall" in Christianity, humanity gradually descended into sin and depravity, but through it all, never lost knowledge of the basic laws of morality and the small voice of conscience giving them the knowledge of sin and wrong-doing.

Humans have a dual nature – material (animal) and spiritual. Thus we have passions and feelings belonging to both realms. The soul, made in God's image, is what makes us into the greatest of the divine creations. The material (animal) inclinations only become sinful if they violate the laws of God (1 John 3:4). When that happens, the spiritual aspirations become dormant and the soul becomes encrusted with evil. Since humans have a free will, each person can choose which of the two natures will predominate in their life. They can align with the spiritual mind and divine image in their souls and thus strengthen their spiritual nature; or they can indulge in sinful thoughts and actions, through which the soul becomes contaminated (Rom. 7:14-8:2; 8:5-8 [4]; 1 Pet. 2:11[5]).

Since the Fall or rebellion against God, humanity has largely followed the animal nature, resulting in what the Bible calls the "works of the flesh," "desires of the sinful nature," or lusts and wrong motives leading to wars and animosities (Gal. 5:16-21; James 3:14-16; 4:1-8[6]) – its present natural state.

Chapter 4: Natural Human State and Origin of Evil

Nature of Man

Man consists of a physical body, soul, and spirit body. Each is made of a different substance, has a different function, and functions for a different length of time.

The physical body is material and temporary. After the end of the physical life, it will dissolve into its constituent elements and never again be resurrected in a physical form. Its function is to shield the soul and spirit body during the earthly life. The body continually changes as cells die and are replaced, but its identity is basically preserved. This material part is not the real person – the soul is. When its function has been accomplished, the body ceases to be a part of the individual altogether.

The spirit body contains the functions of life and what controls the person's behaviour. This includes the intellect, mental faculties, and reasoning powers. The spirit body uses the organs of the material body to manifest these attributes. However, the spirit faculties can function even when the brain or the physical organs of one or more of the five senses are impaired. This body also contains the life principle which does not die, but continues beyond physical death after dropping the envelope of flesh.

As will be discussed in more detail in the next chapter, after death, each individual soul, now only in a spirit body, goes on living in the spirit world. The mind – the mental and intellectual faculties – also continues, now without the limitations that the physical body had placed on it. Memory and all the things forming an individual's identity likewise continue. The person in the spirit world can still conceive thoughts of material things and perceive the physical – even more perfectly than before.

Origin of Evil

As mentioned, humans were created with both animal appetites and spiritual aspirations, but in the beginning, these were in harmony with the moral laws for human conduct. After the original disobedience, however, people have often exercised their will in wrong ways and against God-ordained laws. They followed their animal desires, which unduly asserted themselves at the expense of their spiritual aspirations, that were partly lost due to the Fall. The perversion of the animal appetites and/or the loss of spiritual aspirations lead to disharmony and sin (cf. James 1:13-15[1]).

Evil and the defilements of the soul are creations of not only the mind, but also of emotions, affections and the intellect. These defilements result in alienation from the good, being opposed to man's original state of perfection. The initial purity of the soul is besmirched by the impurities that the person's misguided animal appetites have created. These impurities then become a part of the individual's being and soul. They keep one in discord with the laws controlling the human existence and result in unhappiness.

The soul in this state can become awakened to its defilements and the fruitless pursuits of worldly values. Upon this realization, the person may then choose to embark on a path to purification of their soul and development of natural love.

Overcoming Sin and Purifying the Soul

The powerful force of the will needs to be used to destroy the acquired soul defilements and impurities. First however, human desires must be controlled and harmonized with God's laws. This again involves the mind, as well as emotions and affections (which are of the soul). Effort must then be directed to replacing the unlawful animal desires which engender sin with desires that are in harmony with God's laws and lead to purification of the natural human love and to happiness.

While humans can strive for recapturing the original state of purity, which aligns one with God's laws and will, it does not mean that they are divine, at one with God, or that God is within their soul. The soul was only made in the image of God. However, it does have the potential for being transformed from the divine image into divine substance. This occurs through asking for and receiving the Divine Love into the soul, which is imparted by the Holy Spirit. At this point, the person begins to acquire

Natural Human State and Origin of Evil

divine nature and ultimately immortality (2 Pet. 1:3-4[2]; 2 Tim. 1:9-10[3]). This transformation from human to divine is the greatest of all miracles.

If humans do not overcome their sinful nature in this life, they pass into the spirit world in their evil state and end up in one of the hell realms. They will have opportunities to learn the truth and progress towards perfection and the heavenly realms. Some, however, remain in their sin and wickedness for a long time and may also influence humans on the earth towards evil. They are perceived as devils or demons, but in reality, there is no personal "Satan", but only spirits of departed evil mortals from a humanly unseen world influencing the earth inhabitants by suggesting sinful thoughts and desires to them.

Individuals who have passed into the spirit world (each now being a soul in a spirit body) do not again incarnate (reincarnate). In fact, the conditions on earth are less conducive to spiritual progress than those in the spirit world. Karma (cause and effect or the result of one's actions) doesn't need to take place in a physical body, and purification or progression can continue in the spirit world.

Chapter 5: Beyond Death

After physical death, humans don't cease to live – they merely enter life on a different plane and in different form, becoming inhabitants of the spirit world.

When Death Comes

At death, the so-called silver cord, which bonds the physical body and spirit body together, is broken and the connection is severed for all eternity (Eccl. 12:6-7[1]). When this happens, nothing can resuscitate the person back to life. The lifeless physical body disintegrates over time. It has fulfilled its purpose and will never again be used by the same individual, or another spirit or soul.

The Bible mentions several individuals that Jesus is said to have raised back to life – Lazarus, Jairus' daughter, and a widow's son (Luke 7:11-15; 8:41-42, 49-56; John 11:4, 11-44). In view of the fact that once the silver cord is severed, resuscitation with the soul returning to the physical body is impossible, these individuals weren't truly dead, but only appeared so from the human perspective. More accurately, they would have been in a state of suspended animation. And indeed, Jesus said to the mourners on two of these occasions: "This sickness [of Lazarus] will not end in death." (John 11:4); and "[Jairus' daughter] is not dead but asleep" (Luke 8:52).

Interestingly and by contrast, Jesus after his crucifixion was dead. However, when he appeared to the disciples after his "resurrection", they at first didn't recognize him (Luke 24:13-35; John 20:14-18). The reason, according to subsequent revelation, is that he appeared in a new body which, through the power he possessed as a result of the great amount of Divine Love in his soul, he was able to create from the elements of the universe. Through the same power, he was able to dematerialize his original body, making it disappear from the tomb. (For more details on this, see Further Reading for this chapter.)

Passing into the Spirit World

The passage into the spirit world happens through a "resurrection" of the spirit body which also contains the soul. The spirit body remaining after death has a real substance. It doesn't need and cannot be clothed with another physical body as this would contravene the laws operating on earth, as well as those in the spirit world.

Individuals who have passed into the spirit world retain all the things of mind, conscience and soul that were theirs in the earthly life. The spirit body continues to house, protect and control the soul. To some degree, the soul also controls the spirit body. Changes in the body occur over time, but are not controlled by the laws that control the changes in the physical body, but rather by laws which control the development or purification of the soul.

When an individual, now spirit, first enters the spirit world, it is met by loving family or friends, who help it to awaken to its new existence and adjust to the new environment. When the spirit realizes its new state, it then needs to move to where it is destined based on its soul condition and its mental and moral development in accordance with the Law of Attraction.

Based on the Law of Compensation (also known as cause and effect or karma), a contaminated soul cannot have a place in the Spiritual Heavens or Paradise, (much less the Celestial Heavens or Kingdom of God) unless it is purified. This process will involve a period of suffering in the lower regions or hells. The time this will take depends on the soul itself – its will and awakening – as well as the help of other spirits. Spirits of similar condition assist one another – somewhat like the blind leading the blind. All spirits have work to do and opportunity to grow and progress to higher realms. Eventually all souls will become cleansed and reach the point of their original purity. Those who have sought and received the Divine Love will progress to the Kingdom of God in the Celestial Spheres.

Most spirits find their initial habitation on the earth plane, in which there are several spheres. Here conditions are not too different from those on earth with the same ideas of right and wrong, beliefs, concepts, and desires. Friends and relatives can help and instruct the newly arrived spirit on how to proceed higher. Depending on the spirit's soul condition as well as priorities, they will

Chapter 6: Jesus' Life and Message of Salvation

In contrast to what the gospels describe regarding Jesus' supernatural and virgin birth, I present an alternative view that makes more sense to me. I would also like to point out that the idea of a virgin birth is not a first or unique to Christianity, but is commonly found especially in Asiatic religions. Examples include, among many others, Krishna, Buddha, Lao-Tzu, and to some, even Plato. It appears that often the disciples of a great spiritual leader subsequently concluded that somehow that person was an incarnated god. Jesus was unique among humans and had a special mission, but he was not God. It will be shown in what ways he possessed a divine nature and how we can all follow in his footsteps.

Jesus came to the earth like any other human being – born from the physical union of a man and a woman – Joseph and Mary. He was not born equal to God or as God in human flesh with the substance of God, and thus is not God.

However, he was born with a pure soul, constituted to know the Father, as was originally given to the first parents, and unencumbered by inherited tendencies to sin that we all have. He had a deeply spiritual nature and consequently, from his infancy it was natural for his soul to yearn for at-onement with the Father, and as a result, receive Divine Love.

Throughout his childhood, adolescence and into adulthood, his soul had undergone a transformation from just divine image into divine substance, and he enjoyed close communions with God and an ever-growing at-onement with Him. As a result, he was able to live without sin. With his soul being transformed into divine substance, he was both human and divine – but not equal to the Father or member of a divine Trinity.

Jesus' earthly mission was revealed to him as he progressed in his soul development. However, it was not until his anointing, with the baptism by his cousin John, that he was qualified to start his work (Matt. 3:1-17). At this point, he became the messiah or Christ – which is that part of Jesus, the spirit of truth, which manifests the existence of the Divine Love in the soul.

Jesus' Mission

Jesus' mission was twofold, namely: to declare to humankind that the Father had re-bestowed the Divine Love which Adam and Eve, or the first parents, had forfeited; and to show humans the way by which that Love could be obtained, so that the possessor of it would partake of divine nature and immortality, which can only come from God (2 Pet. 1:3-4 [1]; 1 Tim. 6:15-16 [2]).

In other words, Jesus came to reveal that the Divine Love with its potential of immortality was again available to humans as well as to spirits (deceased mortals who have passed into the spirit world). This privilege had been lost when the first humans chose to disobey God and go their own way. Jesus not only taught this truth, also referred to as the New Birth (John 1:13; 3:3-7), but lived it as his soul was filled with the Divine Love. Thus he brought immortality and eternal life to light (2 Tim. 1:10 [3]). He should be honoured for this, but not worshipped as God or a member of the Godhead or Trinity. Worship belongs only to God the Father (Luke 4:8; John 17:3).

Jesus never claimed that he came to earth to pay any ransom for humans, or to save them by his death on the cross, or to save them in any other way than by teaching them that the great gift or privilege of immortality had been bestowed upon them, and that by prayer and faith they could obtain it.

Jesus' blood and death, or the belief therein, does not reconcile humans to God. Neither is this accomplished through any specific commandment keeping, such as Sabbath observance (which among others is a valuable spiritual discipline). For a full reconciliation to God to occur, the soul has to be developed and only the Divine Love, imparted through the Holy Spirit, can bring this about. It transforms the soul from the image of God into the very essence of God – a redeemed child of God partaking of divine substance (in contrast to only being a child of God through the creation of soul, which is true of all humans).

Jesus is coming again, but not in a physical form to wage war and conquer God's enemies. Rather, he is coming in the form of revelation. His teachings about the Divine Love through the Holy Spirit are entering receptive souls around the world. His desire is that humans turn away from their evil thoughts and ways, and seek the Love and mercy of the Father.

So to recap, Jesus is the saviour not by paying a supposed debt to God by his blood and death, but rather by bringing to light and showing the way to eternal life and immortality. He was the first to receive the Divine Love and become, at the soul level, divine himself – though not God. Thus he became the first fruit of the resurrection (Acts 26:22-23 [4]; 1 Cor. 15:20-23).

Everyone on earth and the spirit world can choose to follow Jesus' example – the only way to unison and at-onement with the Father and access to the heavenly mansions of God's Kingdom. Seeking soul transformation through the Divine Love so that the human soul becomes like God's Soul and a partaker of the divine qualities of Love and life is an individual pursuit, because salvation is individual. Each person is responsible for their own growth (Phil 2:12-13).

In other words, the plan of salvation – the only way a person can be saved from their sins is through the New

Birth as Jesus pointed out to Nicodemus (John 3:3-8). This is the result of the Divine Love flowing into the human soul. As the soul becomes filled with the Love of the Father, everything that tends to sin and error will be absorbed by the Love and disappear. The Love spreads like leaven through dough and the person becomes like the Father in divine nature and fit to inhabit God's Celestial Kingdom (Matt. 13:33; 2 Pet. 1:3-4).

As some become filled with the Divine Love, they will begin to understand the laws governing the relationship of spirit to material world. As a result, they will be able to perform miracles like Jesus did, such as healings. They will point others to the way to realize the greatest of all miracles, which is the transformation of the human soul into divine essence through Divine Love imparted by the Holy Spirit.

Jesus' past and present mission is to call humans to turn to God and to pursue a way of peace and mutual love. This is a soul process. Therefore Jesus is not involved in wars and scenes of carnage – on the battlefield, souls are generally not open to the influence of Jesus' teachings. Other spirits are designated to help those who have met a violent death to make their transition into the spirit world less violent.

War is never a way to peace, and as long as humans remain in their condition of sin, there will be no peace. Even the horror of war will not prevent future wars. Jesus is not coming to subdue enemies through a bloody war at Armageddon (or elsewhere).

However, each individual soul is in a battle between sin and righteousness (Rom. 7:14-25). Not all souls are winning this battle and hence many dead souls are entering the spirit world. A dead soul needs much help to be awakened to life and this awakening is like rising from death to life. That, in one sense, is a resurrection.

The awakened or "risen" soul can then begin, with its cooperation, to be transformed from sin to purity and develop its natural love, and then progress from natural love to receiving the Divine Love through prayer. Alternatively, it can accelerate its development by praying for the Divine Love upon awakening. This Love will no longer permit hatred and wars and is the only way peace will be brought about (1 John 3:2-9[5)]).

Chapter 7: Prayer for Divine Love

The following is a sample prayer for the receipt of the Divine Love. It doesn't have to be prayed verbatim, but it can give ideas how to approach the Father who is always happy when His children ask for His Holy Spirit which imparts the Divine Love (see Luke 11:13[1]).

In effect, the prayer contains the basic truths given to humankind by Celestial Spirits. One person used the following analogy: Praying with those precious words, thought by thought, is like appreciating the beauty of a crystal chandelier, many little crystals of divine truth that we behold in our meditations, and throughout our day.

This longer, formal prayer can be substituted by personal heartfelt prayers and, as one goes about their daily tasks and becomes aware of God during their day, brief requests expressing the soul's desire for the Divine Love can be uttered at any time or place.

****

Our Father, who are in heaven, we recognize that You are all holy and loving and merciful, and that we are Your children, and not the subservient, sinful and depraved creatures that our false teachers would have us believe. (Matt. 6:9; 1 John 4:8, 16)

Prayer for Divine Love

That we are the greatest of Your creation, and the most wonderful of all Your handiworks, and the objects of Your great Soul's Love and tenderest care. (Psalm 139:13-18[2])

That Your will is that we become at one with You, and partake of Your great Love which You have bestowed upon us through Your mercy and desire that we become, in truth, Your children, through Love, and not through the sacrifice and death of any one of Your creatures. (John 17:11, 20-26).

We pray that You will open up our souls to the inflowing of Your Love, and that then may come Your Holy Spirit to bring into our souls this, Your Love in great abundance, until our souls shall be transformed into the very essence of Yourself; and that there may come to us faith – such faith as will cause us to realize that we are truly Your children and one with You in very substance and not in image only. (1 John 4:7, 12-13[3], 16-17)

Let us have such faith as will cause us to know that You are our Father, and the bestower of every good and perfect gift, and that only we, ourselves, can prevent Your Love changing us from the mortal to the immortal. (Jas 1:17-18[4])

Let us never cease to realize that Your Love is waiting for each and all of us, and that when we come to You, in faith and earnest aspiration, Your Love will never be withheld from us. (Luke 11:13)

Keep us in the shadow of Your Love every hour and moment of our lives, and help us to overcome all temptations of the flesh, and the influence of the powers of the evil ones, which so constantly surround us and endeavour to turn our thoughts away from You to the pleasures and allurements of this world. (Matt. 6:13; Jas 1:13-15)

We thank You for Your Love and the privilege of receiving it, and we believe that You are our Father — the loving Father who smiles upon us in our weakness, and is always ready to help us and take us into Your arms of Love. (Luke 15:11-32)

We pray this with all the earnestness and longings of our souls, and trusting in Your Love, give You all the glory and honour and love that our finite souls can give. Amen. (1 Tim. 1:17)

Chapter 8: Divine Love versus Natural Love

God is Love and no human can come into His presence unless they have His Love, the Divine Love in their soul. This Love redeems humans from the way of sin and error that they are prone to as a result of the inherited tendency to sin, and from sin's consequences in the spirit world. The Divine Love can be freely obtained through a sincere prayer in response to the longings of the soul (not just the desires of the mind and intellect), and faith that the Father will bestow it. The intellect cannot unite a person with God – only the soul, made in divine image or likeness, can make this connection. However, the likeness is only perfected by filling the soul with the Divine Love of the Father.

Love makes the whole universe run in harmony – without it, all would be chaos and unhappiness. Only the Divine Love can unite God and humans, and enable humans to become divine angels with access to an abode in the Celestial Spheres.

The Holy Spirit is the sole instrument that can bring about the salvation of man by imparting the Divine Love. Without the Holy Spirit, no one can be forgiven, become an immortal child of God by having their soul transformed into divine substance, and enter the Celestial Heaven. Resisting and rejecting the influence of the Holy Spirit consists of sin against the Spirit and as long as this persists, the person cannot be forgiven – it becomes the unforgivable sin (Matt. 12:32; Rom. 8:6-17[(1)]).

The Divine Love is an unconditional love regardless of the status of another being. It is the Love with which God loves the world. Jesus taught his disciples to love one another with the love that he had for them – which was the same as the Love that the Father loved him with (John 13:34-35; 15:9-13; 17:23). He also taught them to love and pray for their enemies. Doing this, they would approach the perfection of the Father, who showers favours on both the just and the unjust (Matt. 5:44-48). Growing in the likeness of the Father and having their souls transformed from the image of God into divine substance, they would be becoming more and more at one with God.

Human love is a mere shadow or image of the Divine Love. It is the love we are born with and develop as we grow up. It is manifested through, for example, motherly love, sibling love, married love, and love for friends. In expressing love to God, it is in obeying God's commandments (Deut. 10:12) – but may not go much beyond that as shown by the example of the rich young man who asked Jesus what was needed to inherit eternal life. The natural love is not sufficient to enter the Kingdom of God – which is humanly impossible and can only come through God's help in the form of the Divine Love imparted by the Holy Spirit and resulting in soul transformation and the New Birth (Matt. 19:16-26).

The natural love needs to be absorbed and replaced by the Divine Love in order for the soul of a person to be transformed into divine essence. If humans, both in their physical life and after death, when they enter the spirit world, refuse to ask for and receive the Divine Love, they will remain separated from the Father. As a result, they will only experience the limited happiness – though great from their perspective – that the natural love affords them. In time, however, they will also reach a limit to their growth and development, and in addition to their happiness, also experience a certain dissatisfaction. If they are not awakened to the need for the Divine Love, there is nothing divine in them and they will remain in this state with no assurance of immortality or even continuous life. Of course, their existence is sustained by the creating and life-giving Spirit – which is not God, but emanating from God – the universal energy or life force and consciousness in and behind all things (Acts 17:27-28).

It is possible for all to seek and receive the Divine Love, but each individual needs to ask for It. Because of the God-given free will, many will not choose the way of seeking this Love. Also, there may come a time when the privilege of obtaining the Divine Love will be withdrawn.

The harmony of the universe is not dependent upon all humans / spirits receiving the Divine Love (and many may not). This is because in the workings of God's laws of harmony on individual souls, all sin and error will eventually be eradicated and only truth will remain.

However, the absence of sin doesn't mean that all will be equally happy. Those with only the natural love will not be as happy as those with the Divine Love. Yet despite these differences, there will be overall harmony throughout.

Adam and Eve had the natural love and were relatively happy, but couldn't resist temptation. Those in the spirit world with only the natural love too may be subject to temptation and, if it is not resisted, to fall from their state of happiness. By contrast, those with the Divine Love, whose souls have been transformed into divine substance, become a part of divinity. As a result they will never be subject to temptation or unhappiness. They are destined to live as immortal sinless divine angels through all eternity in the presence of and at-one with the Father.

Chapter 9: Divine Love in the Bible

Some readers may be shocked at the teaching about salvation through the receiving of the Divine Love rather than by the vicarious atonement through Jesus' death on the cross. This chapter shows that the Bible, while containing many references to being saved by the sacrifice of Jesus, also has just as many references to the transformation of the heart, becoming a new creature, acquiring divine nature, undergoing a New Birth, experiencing the Divine Love, and other related concepts. Let's go and explore.

Jesus was born as the prophesied Messiah or the anointed one. While the Jews expected a Messiah's coming based on ancient prophecies, they were hoping for a conqueror who would free Judea from Roman domination and set up an earthly kingdom. While Jesus came as a king, his kingdom was not of this world (John 18:36). Rather, it was the Kingdom of God – a Celestial Kingdom of Divine Love. The anointing that Jesus received involved God bestowing His Divine Love into Jesus' soul by means of His Holy Spirit. This was God's gift given first to Jesus, but thereafter available to all who would ask for it with sincere and heartfelt prayer. Thus Jesus was the first of many brethren to become a true child of God (Rom. 8:29), whose soul was transformed by the Divine Love from divine image into divine substance.

The message of the Divine Love that Jesus brought became lost in the copying and rewriting of the present biblical texts, but traces of it can be seen throughout, in the same way that traces of other teachings of Jesus and the early Christians are apparent.

Indeed, the New Testament gospels, written decades after the events they describe, contain several intertwining messages. This is the result of historical events being perceived and recorded by various individuals, as well as follow-up reinterpretations and editing by later writers and editors whose thinking and prejudices also found their way into the texts. This chapter addresses two of the threads – namely the *message of Jesus* versus a later *message about Jesus*.

Jesus' Teaching

Key thoughts of the *message that Jesus brought* deal with the availability of Divine Love (imparted by the Holy Spirit) as follows:

1. God is love (1 John 4:8, 16). This Divine Love (Greek *agape*) transcends the natural human love, which at its best can include unconditional acceptance and lofty deeds.

2. God's Love was displayed by sending Jesus (1 John 4:9) and through him the message that the Divine Love and nature is available to humans as a gift for the

asking. This was also the message that God's Kingdom was near (Matt. 4:17). Through acquiring the Divine Love, by which the individual will would align with divine will, the way to God's Kingdom (the Celestial Spheres) was open (Matt. 7:21).

3. Jesus, as the Messiah (Christ or anointed) was the first to experience the New Birth that he taught about. He manifested the Divine Love, received through the Holy Spirit, and set an example of a life motivated by this Love (Matt. 11:29). While his countrymen expected him to establish an earthly kingdom and overthrow the Romans, Jesus taught that his kingdom was not visible in the ordinary sense. Yet, the kingdom was *among them* – through his person, and could be *within them* – by receiving the Divine Love in their souls as he had (Matt. 17:21 – the Greek word can have both meanings).

4. Those who in their soul desire the gift of the Divine Love and sincerely pray for it will receive it and have their soul transformed from divine image into divine substance. This is the New Birth – being born again of imperishable seed or being born of God (John 1:13; 3:3, 5; Titus 3:5; 1 Peter 1:23; 1 John 4:7-9).

5. Jesus practiced and taught love for one another (1 John 3:11). The apostle John, who among the disciples was spiritually the closest to Jesus, later showed how if we truly love one another and walk as Jesus did, God, through His Love, lives in us and we in Him, and His Love is made complete in us (1 John 2:5-6; 4:12, 16). The Divine Love transforming our souls gives us the knowledge of our unity (at-onement) with the Father (John 17:20-26).

6. The Holy Spirit is a spirit of power, love and self-control (Acts 1:8; 2 Tim. 1:7). Jesus and his disciples manifested the gift of the Divine Love by the power to heal (e.g., Matt. 4:23; 12:15; 14:14; Mark 1:30-34; 6:55-56; 8:22-25; Luke 8:27-29, 41-48; 9:38-42). Empowered through the Divine Love, the disciples were sent out on their mission two by two to heal and preach the gospel of the Kingdom of God (Mark 6:7-13; Luke 9:1-2, 6; Luke 10:1-17). However, it was on the day of Pentecost that the promise of the Father occurred and the Holy Spirit came and delivered the Divine Love in great abundance. Then the apostles were able to do even greater works (Acts 2:1-43; 3:3-8; 5:12-16).

7. Jesus also used parables to help people understand the preciousness of this powerful, yet invisible gift, comparing it to a treasure or a pearl of great value worth all that one has (Matt. 13:44-46). He also showed its power to transform through the parables of the mustard seed and yeast in a batch of dough (Matt. 13:31-32). He taught that the Father is more willing to grant this gift to His children than earthly parents enjoy giving good gifts to their offspring (Luke 11:13).

8. The gift of the Divine Love is referred to in the New Testament as

- Gift of grace (2 Cor. 9:15)
- Salvation by grace (not because of good deeds), through the washing of rebirth / New Birth and renewal by the Holy Spirit (Tit. 3:5)
- Participation in the divine nature (2 Pet. 1:4)

- God's glory (in the form of divine nature); it unites those who possess it and through their lives makes God known to those who don't (John 17:20-26)
- Experiencing the fullness of God (Eph. 3:19)
- Power that works in us (Eph. 3:20)
- Power of God for salvation and righteousness of God by faith (Rom. 1:16-17)
- God's light shining in our hearts to give us the knowledge of the glory of God (2 Cor. 4:6)
- Source of life and immortality (2 Tim. 1:10)
- Love poured into our hearts by the Holy Spirit (Rom. 5:5)
- Love that surpasses all other spiritual gifts, as well as knowledge (1 Cor. 13:1-3; Eph. 3:18-19)
- Being rooted and established in love (Eph. 3:17)
- Gift of the Holy Spirit, the spirit of grace (Luke 11:13; Acts 10:45, Heb. 10:29)
- Streams of living waters — the received Holy Spirit (John 7:38-39; 20:22) Note: In the Old Testament, God is metaphorically called the spring of living water (Jer. 2:13; 17:13)
- Living water permanently quenching [spiritual] thirst and becoming a spring welling up to eternal life (John 4:10-14)
- Spirit in our inner being (heart or soul) (Eph. 3:16; 2 Tim. 1:14), motivating us to do what is right (Rom. 7:22)

Divine Love in the Bible

- Spirit of love and other God-like qualities that transcend the law (Gal. 5:22-23)
- Spirit in our hearts as a deposit for our glorious future in God's Kingdom (2 Cor. 1:22)
- Spirit which makes us children of the Father and at one with Him, as well as heirs of divine glory (Rom. 8:9, 14-17)
- Anointing (1 John 2:20-27; 2 Cor. 1:21)
- Christ [the anointing that came with Jesus] dwelling in our hearts through faith (Eph. 3:17)
- Christ in us, the hope of glory (Col. 1:27)
- Being in Christ and becoming a new creation (2 Cor. 5:17; Gal. 6:15)
- Conversion through having the door of faith opened by God (Acts 14:27; 15:3)
- Being transformed and made new by the renewing of the mind (Rom 12:2; Eph. 4:23)
- Putting on the new self to be like God in righteousness and holiness (Eph. 4:24)
- Walking in the Spirit (Gal. 5:16, 25)
- Loving one another as a result of God-given Love, through which we know God and are born of God (1 John 4:7-8)

In addition to the above, many biblical references to the *Holy Spirit can be seen as synonymous with Divine Love* in that the Spirit, like the Divine Love, is a means of conversion, new life, new heart, becoming a new creation / creature, salvation, and resurrection to immortality.

Another "Gospel"

In addition to the *message about the Divine Love that Jesus preached and lived*, the gospel books and other New Testament writings contain a second "gospel" – *about Jesus* and emphasizing *his death by crucifixion which is said to have paid the penalty for our sins* (e.g., Rom. 3:25; Eph. 5:2; Heb. 7:27; 9:12-14; 26-28; 10:11-12; 1 John 2:2; 4:10). In contrast to Jesus' own message, this one was introduced by others who subsequently tried to make sense of and explain the "impermissible" death of the Messiah. Jesus as the Messiah was expected to overthrow the Romans, not be killed by them – despite the fact that Jesus stressed that his kingdom was not of this world (John 18:36). His unexpected death then became interpreted as a part of God's plan in providing a sacrifice for sin and a vicarious atonement.

In keeping with the interpretation of Jesus' death, authors and editors of New Testament books reframed the narratives of his life to conform to these ideas. Words were placed in Jesus' mouth and Hebrew Scriptures misquoted or quoted out of context to substantiate the concept of Jesus as a "sacrificial lamb" (John 1:29; 1 Cor. 5:7; 1 Pet. 1:18-19).

The conflict between the two messages or "gospels" is that on the one hand, God's Love and salvation is a gift from a loving and merciful Father, while on the other hand, the gift first had to be paid for as a ransom to satisfy a wrathful God. These ideas are also incompatible in that Jesus (as God) would have had to pay for his own gift with his life or pay for the Father's gift – in which case it would have been a gift from Jesus, not the Father. Yet Jesus teaches that the gift of salvation is given by God (John 4:10). In addition, God owns everything and can bestow gifts and absolve debts (Luke 15:21-24) – without requiring a sacrifice.

While Jesus travelled from town to town preaching, his message always dealt with present matters, not with his future death as a payment for sin. Rather the Kingdom of God and the New Birth were available in the present (John 3:1-8; Luke 4:21).

The often quoted verse of John 3:16 stating that "God so loved the world that He *gave* His one and only Son, that whoever believes in Him shall not perish but have eternal life" is interesting in the use of the word "gave" – possibly changed by the editors as in the next verse, verse 17[1], and a related passage in 1 John 4:9-17[2] use the word "sent". So John 3:16 would read better as "God so loved the world that He *sent* His Son, that whoever *believes him* [his teachings] shall not perish but have eternal life" Alternatively, "God so loved the world that He gave us *His Divine Love, that whoever receives it* shall not perish but have eternal life."

In summary, there is no efficacy in Jesus' blood to save or pay for human sins and reconcile people to the Father. Those who believe in Jesus Christ's death as a means of their salvation may be neglecting the one vital requirement, and that is the New Birth. This and this only saves humans from their sins and fits them to enter the Kingdom of God, which is the kingdom of Jesus, for he is the Prince of that kingdom, and the master and ruler thereof.

Chapter 10: Immortal Divine Angels

Humans have sensed for centuries that there is more to life than the brief physical existence between birth and death – and this is true. Life continues in the spirit world with a spirit body after the physical body had been left behind in death. There is, however, a difference between the condition of a human soul in the spirit world just continuing its life, and a state where the extinction of life is an utter impossibility – even by God who, in the beginning of man's existence, created that soul. True immortality is the state of the soul which knows that because of the divine essence and qualities of itself, it can never cease to live.

What applies on earth to created things having a beginning and an end – being dissolved into their elements – can also be true in the spirit world. Death is the process through which change from humanly visible to invisible occurs – the physical becomes spirit. This, however, of and by itself doesn't guarantee everlasting existence. It is because the soul in the physical body is the same when it enters the spirit world. It had a beginning and is not self-existing or independent, and thus must rely on God's will and sustenance by the Spirit of God for its continued existence.

Immortality can only be acquired from that which is immortal – it is not inherent in any created thing. Only God is immortal (1 Tim. 6:15-16), which means that His nature and qualities are immortal. The most important quality is Love – without it, God could not be God. In whatever the Divine Love enters, this being receives immortality – and it cannot receive immortality any other way. Whoever receives immortality can never die or cease to exist – they have passed beyond the "second death". They are now divine angels, having had their soul transformed from a divine image into divine substance.

Immortal divine angels inhabit the Celestial Spheres, or Kingdom of God. Their soul qualities mirror the Father's divine nature. The angels can continue to grow in the Divine Love and perfection till they get into the presence of the Father and are able to see Him with their ever-increasing and clearer soul perceptions.

The angels are now ministering to unredeemed humans and spirits. (This is also true of the perfected spirits in the spheres below the Celestial Kingdom.). Having had the experience of physical human existence with its accompanying sorrows, as well as that of redemption from their condition of sin and error, they love and can fully understand those they are serving. Even Jesus lived in a physical body, enabling him to understand the frailties, sufferings and longings of mortals. This labour of love towards the unredeemed brings the divine angels joy – especially when they see results.

The Bible mentions other angels who haven't had the human experience, but they reside in other parts of heaven and are not involved with the work of human salvation. The divine angels in the Celestial Spheres are happy beyond human conception. Even though they are not dissatisfied in any way, the Law of Progression works with them so that they continue to long for higher life and seek for greater abundance of the Divine Love. So there is both perfect happiness and desire to progress to achieve fuller happiness.

While the world is full of false doctrines and beliefs which retard the soul's progress and keep many from the Light (Col. 2:8[1]; 2 John 1:7), there are also truths scattered throughout the various teachings and philosophies which show the way to the Celestial Kingdom of God. Those who understand God's Love and Jesus' teachings can grasp the real Truth of redemption once they learn it. A time is coming when the Truth will be universally taught, humanity will live in happiness, and the Kingdom of Heaven will exist on earth. The opportunity for redemption through the Divine Love will then be universally taught (Isa. 11:6-9; Hab. 2:14[2]).

Epilogue

This book has presented a fresh, non-traditional look at the Bible and Christian orthodox teachings. If the concepts presented here resonate with you and make sense, you have an exciting spiritual journey before you and a glorious destiny to work toward.

Adherents to all major religious traditions seek to find meaning to their life, both here and beyond. Most acknowledge the existence of a Higher Power as they understand it – the Source of all that is. Divine Love, the essence of a loving Creator God, transcends all religions. If these teachings are true, they can be seen as the only religion – and the universal way to God and salvation (as opposed to the traditional belief that people have to become Christians and accept Jesus' sacrifice for their sins before they can be saved).

In a way, these teachings can be integrated into the different religions. Believers of various persuasions, who already strive for a life of love, morality, and ethics can adopt them, and have their souls transformed by the Divine Love. If and when this happens, their very partial understanding of the ultimate reality (which we all have) will also gradually grow.

People of different faiths hope and believe that this life is not all there is. If that's the case, it behoves all of us to gain more understanding of the next life and prepare for it here and now. I believe that seeking and growing in the

Epilogue

Divine Love is the best answer. However, each person has to decide for themselves.

Ideally, humans need to ponder these vital truths in this life as the spirit world will not greatly help them of and by itself to obtain a more enlightened insight. A spirit is only a human without a physical body and the accompanying cares. Some retain these cares for a long time after coming to the spirit world and are only relieved of them by paying the penalties of a violated law. However, those spirits who resist the temptations to indulge their previous life passions and appetites are able to turn their thoughts to higher things and may soon realize that only the New Birth brought about by soul transformation through the Divine Love of the Father can help them reach their highest potential and a glorious destiny as immortal divine angels in the Celestial Kingdom of God.

If you are ready to test the truth of the message in this book, why not commit to personally start praying for the Divine Love? Use either the prayer in Chapter 7 or your own sincere and heartfelt prayer. In a few weeks of earnest and consistent prayer, you are likely to notice greater peace and closeness to the Creator, as well as more love, joy, happiness and serenity.

As you continue praying and grow in the Love, your life will become more loving and less stressed. You'll grow in understanding of vital truths. And when your time comes to leave this world and enter the spirit world, you will be well on the way to the Celestial Kingdom of God that Jesus spoke about where unsurpassed bliss and happiness await those who have achieved at-onement with their Heavenly Father through soul transformation from divine image into divine substance by the Divine Love.

Notes and Further Reading

For the readers' convenience, this section includes quotes of selected important Bible texts, as well as providing reading references for those who wish to learn more. The information is organized chapter by chapter.

The New International Version of the Bible is quoted throughout, and the quoted Bible texts are marked in the chapter texts by superscript numbers. Readers are encouraged to check for themselves the scriptural references mentioned in the text which are too numerous to quote here.

The online reading references can be matched with page numbers in the printed volumes of *True Gospel Revealed Anew by Jesus* which are available for free upon request from the Foundation Church of the New Birth at http://www.divinelove.org/.
Contact email: newbirth@divinelove.org).

Chapter 1 – The Bible and Christianity

Sample Bible passages showing scriptural inspiration:

(1) Jeremiah 18:5-6: Then the word of the LORD came to me: "O house of Israel, can I not do with you as this potter does?" declares the LORD. "Like clay in the hand of the potter, so are you in my hand, O house of Israel. . . ."

(2) Hebrews 11:7-8: By faith Noah, when warned about things not yet seen, in holy fear built an ark to save his family. By his faith he condemned the world and became heir of the righteousness that comes by faith. By faith Abraham, when called to go to a place he would later receive as his inheritance, obeyed and went, even though he did not know where he was going.

(3) Luke 24:27: And beginning with Moses and all the Prophets, [Jesus] explained to them what was said in all the Scriptures concerning himself.

(4) John 17:20-23: My prayer is not for them alone. I pray also for those who will believe in me through their message, that all of them may be one, Father, just as you are in me and I am in you. May they also be in us so that the world may believe that you have sent me. I have given them the glory that you gave me, that they may be one as we are one: I in them and you in me. May they be brought to complete unity to let the world know that you sent me and have loved them even as you have loved me.

(5) Philippians 2:12-15: Therefore, my dear friends, as you have always obeyed – not only in my presence, but now much more in my absence – continue to work out your salvation with fear and trembling, for it is God who works in you to will and to act according to his good purpose. Do everything without complaining or arguing, so that you may become blameless and pure, children of God without

fault in a crooked and depraved generation, in which you shine like stars in the universe.

Further Reading
http://new-birth.net/tgrabjvol1/bible29.htm

Chapter 2 – Nature of God

Sample Bible passages in support of the presented concepts:

(1) 1 John 4:8, 16: Whoever does not love does not know God, because God is love. ... And so we know and rely on the love God has for us. God is love. Whoever lives in love lives in God, and God in him.

(2) Ephesians 2:4-5: But because of his great love for us, God, who is rich in mercy, made us alive with Christ even when we were dead in transgressions — it is by grace you have been saved.

(3) Psalm 47:8: God reigns over the nations; God is seated on his holy throne.

(4) Psalm 139:7-12: Where can I go from your Spirit? Where can I flee from your presence? If I go up to the heavens, you are there; if I make my bed in the depths, you are there. If I rise on the wings of the dawn, if I settle on the far side of the sea, even there your hand will guide me, your right hand will hold me fast. If I say, "Surely the darkness will hide me and the light become night around

me," even the darkness will not be dark to you; the night will shine like the day, for darkness is as light to you. For you created my inmost being; you knit me together in my mother's womb.

(5) 1 John 3:1: How great is the love the Father has lavished on us, that we should be called children of God! And that is what we are! The reason the world does not know us is that it did not know him. Dear friends, now we are children of God, and what we will be has not yet been made known. But we know that when he appears, we shall be like him, for we shall see him as he is.

(6) Isaiah 55:7: Let the wicked forsake his way and the evil man his thoughts. Let him turn to the LORD, and he will have mercy on him, and to our God, for he will freely pardon.

Further Reading
http://new-birth.net/tgrabjvol1/god4.htm

Chapter 3 – Early History and Human Origins

Sample Bible passages in support of the presented concepts:

(1) Ecclesiastes 12:6: Remember [God] – before the silver cord is severed, or the golden bowl is broken; before the pitcher is shattered at the spring, or the wheel broken at the well, and the dust returns to the ground it came from, and the spirit returns to God who gave it.

(2) Zechariah 12:1: ... The LORD, who stretches out the heavens, who lays the foundation of the earth, and who forms the spirit of man within him, declares: ...

(3) Ezekiel 11:19: I will give them an undivided heart and put a new spirit in them; I will remove from them their heart of stone and give them a heart of flesh. Then they will follow my decrees and be careful to keep my laws. They will be my people, and I will be their God.

(4) Romans 8:5-8: Those who live according to the sinful nature have their minds set on what that nature desires; but those who live in accordance with the Spirit have their minds set on what the Spirit desires. The mind of sinful man is death, but the mind controlled by the Spirit is life and peace; the sinful mind is hostile to God. It does not submit to God's law, nor can it do so. Those controlled by the sinful nature cannot please God.

(5) 1 Peter 2:11: Dear friends, I urge you, as aliens and strangers in the world, to abstain from sinful desires, which war against your soul.

(6) James 4:1-4: What causes fights and quarrels among you? Don't they come from your desires that battle within you? You want something but don't get it. You kill and covet, but you cannot have what you want. You quarrel and fight. You do not have, because you do not ask God. When you ask, you do not receive, because you ask with wrong motives, that you may spend what you get on your pleasures. You adulterous people, don't you know that

friendship with the world is hatred toward God? Anyone who chooses to be a friend of the world becomes an enemy of God.

Further Reading
http://new-birth.net/tgrabjvol2/ancient3.htm
http://new-birth.net/tgrabjvol2/ancient1.htm
http://new-birth.net/tgrabjvol1/genesis6.htm

Chapter 4 – Humans and Origin of Sin

Bible passages in support of the presented concepts:

(1) James 1:13: When tempted, no one should say, "God is tempting me." For God cannot be tempted by evil, nor does he tempt anyone; but each one is tempted when, by his own evil desire, he is dragged away and enticed. Then, after desire has conceived, it gives birth to sin; and sin, when it is full-grown, gives birth to death.

(2) 2 Peter 1:3: His divine power has given us everything we need for life and godliness through our knowledge of him who called us by his own glory and goodness. Through these he has given us his very great and precious promises, so that through them you may participate in the divine nature and escape the corruption in the world caused by evil desires.

(3) 2 Timothy 1:9-10: ... This grace was given us in Christ Jesus before the beginning of time, but it has now been revealed through the appearing of our Savior, Christ

Jesus, who has destroyed death and has brought life and immortality to light through the gospel.

Further Reading
http://new-birth.net/tgrabjvol2/bible6.htm
http://new-birth.net/tgrabjvol2/bible47.htm
http://new-birth.net/tgrabjvol2/bible41.htm
http://new-birth.net/tgrabjvol1/bible35.htm
http://new-birth.net/tgrabjvol1/hell22.htm

Chapter 5 – Beyond Death

Bible passages in support of the presented concepts:

(1) Ecclesiastes 12:6-7: Remember [God] – before the silver cord is severed, or the golden bowl is broken; before the pitcher is shattered at the spring, or the wheel broken at the well, and the dust returns to the ground it came from, and the spirit returns to God who gave it.

(2) Matthew 18:3-4: And [Jesus] said: "I tell you the truth, unless you change and become like little children, you will never enter the kingdom of heaven. Therefore, whoever humbles himself like this child is the greatest in the kingdom of heaven."

(3) John 3:3, 6: ... Jesus declared, "I tell you the truth, no one can see the kingdom of God unless he is born again. ... Flesh gives birth to flesh, but the Spirit gives birth to spirit."

Further Reading
http://new-birth.net/tgrabjvol2/heaven18.htm
http://new-birth.net/tgrabjvol1/hell16.htm
http://new-birth.net/misc/misc10.htm
http://new-birth.net/tgrabjvol3/minor358.htm
http://new-birth.net/tgrabjvol2/minor156.htm
http://new-birth.net/tgrabjvol1/jesus13.htm

Chapter 6 – Jesus' Life and Message of Salvation

Sample Bible passages in support of the presented concepts:

(1) 2 Peter 1:3-4: His divine power has given us everything we need for life and godliness through our knowledge of him who called us by his own glory and goodness. Through these he has given us his very great and precious promises, so that through them you may participate in the divine nature and escape the corruption in the world caused by evil desires.

(2) 1 Timothy 6:15-16: ... which God will bring about in his own time – God, the blessed and only Ruler, the King of kings and Lord of lords, who alone is immortal and who lives in unapproachable light, whom no one has seen or can see. To him be honor and might forever. Amen.

(3) 2 Timothy 1:10: ... but it has now been revealed through the appearing of our Savior, Christ Jesus, who

has destroyed death and has brought life and immortality to light through the gospel.

(4) Acts 26:22-23: But I have had God's help to this very day, and so I stand here and testify to small and great alike. I am saying nothing beyond what the prophets and Moses said would happen — that the Christ would suffer and, as the first to rise from the dead, would proclaim light to his own people and to the Gentiles.

(5) 1 John 3:9: No one who is born of God will continue to sin, because God's seed remains in him; he cannot go on sinning, because he has been born of God.

Further Reading
http://new-birth.net/ntr/revelation2.htm
http://new-birth.net/tgrabjvol1/divinelove6.htm
http://new-birth.net/ntr/revelation36.htm
http://new-birth.net/tgrabjvol1/bible71.htm
http://new-birth.net/tgrabjvol2/minor156.htm

Chapter 7 – Prayer for the Divine Love

Sample Bible passages in support of the presented concepts:

(1) Luke 11:13: If you then, though you are evil, know how to give good gifts to your children, how much more will your Father in heaven give the Holy Spirit to those who ask him!

(2) Psalm 139:13-14: For you created my inmost being; you knit me together in my mother's womb. I praise you because I am fearfully and wonderfully made; your works are wonderful, I know that full well.

(3) 1 John 4:12-13: No one has ever seen God; but if we love one another, God lives in us and his love is made complete in us. We know that we live in him and he in us, because he has given us of his Spirit.

(4) James 1:17-18: Every good and perfect gift is from above, coming down from the Father of the heavenly lights, who does not change like shifting shadows. He chose to give us birth through the word of truth, that we might be a kind of firstfruits of all he created.

Further Reading
http://new-birth.net/tgrabjvol1/prayer3.htm
http://new-birth.net/prayer4.htm
http://new-birth.net/experiment.htm

Chapter 8 – Divine Love versus Natural Love

Sample Bible passages in support of the presented concepts:

(1) Romans 8:16-17: The Spirit himself testifies with our spirit that we are God's children. Now if we are children, then we are heirs – heirs of God and co-heirs with Christ, if indeed we share in his sufferings in order that we may also share in his glory.

(2) John 15:9-12: As the Father has loved me, so have I loved you. Now remain in my love. If you obey my commands, you will remain in my love, just as I have obeyed my Father's commands and remain in his love. I have told you this so that my joy may be in you and that your joy may be complete. My command is this: Love each other as I have loved you.

(3) Matthew 5:44-45: But I tell you: Love your enemies and pray for those who persecute you, that you may be sons of your Father in heaven. He causes his sun to rise on the evil and the good, and sends rain on the righteous and the unrighteous.

(4) Matthew 19:25-26: When the disciples heard this, they were greatly astonished and asked, "Who then can be saved?" Jesus looked at them and said, "With man this is impossible, but with God all things are possible."

Further Reading
http://new-birth.net/divinelove.htm
http://new-birth.net/tgrabjvol2/divinelove34.htm
http://new-birth.net/tgrabjvol2/divinelove35.htm
http://new-birth.net/tgrabjvol2/bible41.htm
http://new-birth.net/tgrabjvol2/bible42.htm

Chapter 9 – Divine Love in the Bible

I chose to quote only a couple of Bible passages for this chapter as many of the key biblical phrases are already in the text.

(1) John 3:16-17: For God so loved the world that he gave his one and only Son, that whoever believes in him shall not perish but have eternal life. For God did not send his Son into the world to condemn the world, but to save the world through him.

(2) 1 John 4:9-17: This is how God showed his love among us: He sent his one and only Son into the world that we might live through him [his teachings]. This is love: not that we loved God, but that he loved us and sent his Son as an atoning sacrifice for our sins. Dear friends, since God so loved us, we also ought to love one another. No one has ever seen God; but if we love one another, God lives in us and his love is made complete in us. We know that we live in him and he in us, because he has given us of his Spirit. And we have seen and testify that the Father has sent his Son to be the Savior of the world. If anyone acknowledges that Jesus is the Son of God, God lives in him and he in God. And so we know and rely on the love God has for us. God is love. Whoever lives in love lives in God, and God in him. In this way, love is made complete among us so that we will have confidence on the day of judgment, because in this world we are like him.

Further Reading
http://new-birth.net/tgrabjvol1/bible53.htm
http://new-birth.net/tgrabjvol1/bible70.htm
http://new-birth.net/tgrabjvol1/bible71.htm

Chapter 10 – Immortal Divine Angels

Sample Bible passages in support of the presented concepts:

(1) Colossians 2:8: See to it that no one takes you captive through hollow and deceptive philosophy, which depends on human tradition and the basic principles of this world rather than on Christ.

(3) Habakkuk 2:14: ... The earth will be filled with the knowledge of the glory of the LORD, as the waters cover the sea.

Further Reading
http://new-birth.net/tgrabjvol1/heaven16.htm
http://new-birth.net/tgrabjvol2/heaven25.htm

Epilogue

Different people experience the inflowing of the Divine Love into the soul differently. For some testimonials, see http://www.divine-bliss.net/ as well as http://new-birth.net/experiment.htm

References

Books

True Gospel Revealed Anew by Jesus, Volumes 1-4 (Publisher: Foundation Church of the New Birth)

Angelic Revelations of Divine Truth, Volumes 1-2 (Publisher: Foundation Church of Divine Truth)

New Testament Revelations of Jesus of Nazareth (Publisher: Foundation Church of Divine Truth)

Websites

http://new-birth.net/

http://universal-spirituality.net

About the Author

Eva Peck has a Christian and international background. Through Christian work and teaching English as a foreign language in several countries, she has experienced a range of cultures, customs and environments. Having lived and worked in Australia, the United States, Europe, Asia, and the Middle East, she now draws on those experiences in her writing.

Eva refers to biblical passages in this book the way she has come to understand them. Having had the opportunity to fellowship with Christians from a variety of faith traditions, she also recognizes that many faith-related issues can be understood in more than one way.

Eva studied biological sciences as well as theology at the tertiary level and has a Bachelor's degree in Science and a Master's degree in Theology. She lives in Brisbane, Australia, with her husband, Alex.

The Pecks' co-authored books of spiritual nature include *Pathway to Life – through the Holy Scriptures* and *Journey to the Divine Within – through Silence,*

About the Author

Stillness and Simplicity. Both publications, as well as Eva's trilogy *Divine Reflections* and her other books can be ordered through Pathway Publishing. Most of these books are linked to Amazon and available also at other online outlets worldwide.

For more information about Pathway Publishing,
www.pathway-publishing.org
see at the end of the book.

More About the Author's Other Books of Spiritual Nature

Divine Reflections in Times and Seasons

The book looks at times and seasons and explores how every-day phenomena mirror spiritual realities. Readers are encouraged to take a fresh look at a sunrise, the sunlight on trees and flowers, the creatures that cross their path, and the starry heavens, among other things, and contemplate the meaning of it all.

Divine Reflections in Natural Phenomena

This book explores how spiritual realities can be glimpsed in the world of nature – in phenomena such as life and its order, the beauty and harmony around us, and the countless mysteries of the heaven and the earth.

Divine Reflections in Living Things

This volume looks at living organisms among both plants and animals and reflects on the glimpses of the divine in these realms. Readers are encouraged to pause and take a fresh look around them – to see each living creature and every process as if for the first time.

Divine Insights from Human Life

This is a collection of writings drawn from the author's experience. Each begins with a story and is followed by reflections on the wisdom and/or spiritual insights gleaned from the various incidents.

Pathway to Life – Through the Holy Scriptures

Pathway to Life presents in a concise and systematic way the basic teachings of the Bible. It strives to offer a balanced, non-denominational understanding of the Scriptures. Conclusions are supported by scripture references.

Journey to the Divine Within – Through Silence, Stillness and Simplicity

Journey to the Divine Within shares, through the reflections of a variety of spiritual writers, how to enter the realm of one's heart. One way that this occurs is through silence, stillness and simplicity. When pondered, the reflections will lead readers to the silence and stillness of their own hearts on the path to encountering the Life, Light and Love within.

Acknowledgments

First, I would like to thank the Great God, our Heavenly Father, as well as our Celestial guides and teachers for enabling, inspiring, and blessing this small publication.

I am indebted to Rev. Dr. Michael Nedbal, Trustee of Foundation Church of Divine Truth and personal friend, for carefully reviewing my manuscript for doctrinal accuracy and providing helpful comments. I have also appreciated his support and encouragement.

Thanks are also due to the following among my other brothers and sisters in Christ. I especially value the biblical and conceptual input of Marga McCrady. In addition, I am grateful to Al and Jeanne Fike, as well as Terry Adler and Jane Gatshore of Divine Love Sanctuary Foundation, writer and editor Brian Holmes, and David Reed for their support, input, and helpful reviews.

Last, but not least, I wish to thank Alex, my dear husband and best friend for over 40 years, for his love, support of my endeavours, and always being ready to give helpful advice.

Without the support and assistance of these dear souls, this book would not be what it has become. So heartfelt thanks to you all.

About Pathway Publishing

Pathway Publishing is dedicated to sharing truth and beauty by publishing books that present what is true to life and reality, as well as what is lovely and inspirational. The goal is to not only provide sound information, but also to lift the human spirit.

Pathway Publishing has a vision of helping readers on their path of enlightenment and spiritual transformation. The wisdom and experience of spiritual teachers, thinkers and visionary writers from various backgrounds and faith traditions are recognized and valued.

Books produced by Pathway Publishing include books of spiritual nature, as well as books featuring the art, photography and Czech poetry of Eva's father, Jindrich (Henry) Degen, now in his 90s, but still very creative and productive.

- *Divine Reflections in Times and Seasons,* Eva Peck (2013)
- *Divine Reflections in Natural Phenomena,* Eva Peck (2013)
- *Divine Reflections in Living Things,* Eva Peck (2013)
- *Divine Insights from Human Life,* Eva Peck (2013)
- *Pathway to Life - Through the Holy Scriptures,* Eva and Alexander Peck (2011)

- *Journey to the Divine Within – Through Silence, Stillness and Simplicity*, Alex and Eva Peck (2011)
- *Jesus' Gospel of God's Love*, Eva Peck (2015)
- *Artistic Inspirations - Paintings of Jindrich Degen* arranged by Eva and Alexander Peck (2011)
- *Colour and Contrast: Artwork of Jindrich Degen*, arranged by Eva and Alexander Peck (2013)
- *Faces and Forms Across Time: Artwork of Jindrich Degen*, arranged by Eva and Alex Peck (2013)
- *Variations: Art Exhibitions of Jindrich Degen*, arranged by Eva and Alex Peck (2013)
- *Nature in Art: Artwork of Jindrich Degen*, arranged by Eva and Alex Peck (2014)
- *Spirituality in Art: Artwork of Jindrich Degen*, arranged by Eva and Alex Peck (2014)
- *Floral and Nature Art – Photography of Jindrich Degen*, arranged by Eva and Alexander Peck (2011)
- *Nature's Beauty: Art Photography of Jindrich Degen*, arranged by Eva and Alex Peck (2013)
- *Verše pro dnešní dobu (Contemporary Verse)*, Jindrich Degen (in Czech) (2011)
- *Volné verse* (Free Verse), Jindrich Degen (in Czech) (2012)

Some of the publications are also available as e-books.

Pathway Publishing
Seeking truth and beauty

www.ingramcontent.com/pod-product-compliance
Lightning Source LLC
Chambersburg PA
CBHW072102290426

44110CB00014B/1785